10660241

The Greatest Lie

The Greatest Lie

Discover the Truth and Live Forever

By

Michael Youssef, PhD

IPG

Intermedia Publishing Group

The Greatest Lie

Published by:
Intermedia Publishing Group, Inc.
P.O. Box 2825
Peoria, Arizona 85380
www.intermediapub.com

ISBN 978-1-935529-97-2

Copyright © 2010 by Michael Youssef, PhD
Printed in the United States of America

No part of this publication may be reproduced, stored in a retrieval system, or transmitted in any form by any means–electronic, mechanical, digital photocopy, recording, or any other without the prior permission of the author.

All rights reserved solely by the author. The author guarantees all contents are original and do not infringe upon the legal rights of any other person or work. No part of this book may be reproduced in any form without the permission of the author. The views expressed in this book are not necessarily those of the publisher.

All Scripture quotations, unless otherwise indicated, are taken from the *Holy Bible, New International Version®. NIV®*. Copyright © 1973, 1978, 1984 by International Bible Society. Used by permission of Zondervan. All rights reserved.

Table of Contents

Dedication

To Jim and Carolyn Caswell, in deep appreciation for
their encouragement and partnership in the gospel.

Introduction

Decide for Yourself

In 1994, television talk-show host Oprah Winfrey interviewed a woman who claimed to have had a near-death experience. The woman went into great detail explaining how she died and then was brought back to life. During the time she was "dead," Jesus supposedly told her that "all religions are equally true."

After hearing the woman's story, Oprah said, "I believe that there are many paths to God, or many paths to the light. I certainly don't believe that there is only one way. . . . Did Jesus indicate that to you?"

The woman replied, "Yes, absolutely."

"Well," Oprah said, "I'm glad to hear that because if Jesus is as cool as I think He is, He would have had to tell you that."[1]

"Cool" Jesus? Really? Which Jesus? The one this woman hallucinated about or the real Jesus who said the exact opposite during His entire earthly life?

Listen to what Jesus really said in the Scriptures. In John 14:6, the Lord told His disciples, "I am the way and the truth and the life. No one comes to the Father except through me." Jesus makes it clear that He is the only way to heaven. Though many people choose to believe the greatest lie that there are "many paths to the light," Jesus says there is no other path to God except Himself, period.

This is no minor matter. Your entire future—the remainder of your life here on earth as well as your eternal destiny—depends on how you respond to this statement made by the real Jesus Christ. There are many who would want you to believe there are many paths to God. But Jesus said He is the way, the truth, and the life. He wants you to know the danger of believing the greatest lie.

Jesus' message runs counter to what you continually hear on television and radio, in books and magazines, and in conversations with unsaved friends and family members. You are being bombarded on a daily basis with such messages as, "All religions are essentially the same," or "Jesus, Buddha, and Mohammed all teach the same thing."

Do not be misled. I want you to know the truth so you can make up your own mind. As Jesus said to his followers, "If you hold to my teaching, you are really my disciples. Then you will know the truth, and the truth will set you free" (John 8:31-32).

Does it truly matter which path you take? If you are sincere in your beliefs, isn't that enough? No. If Jesus truly is the way, the truth, and the life, but you choose to go a *different* way, then you will arrive at the wrong destination. Being sincere won't help you if you are sincerely wrong.

You don't have to take my word for it. In this book, I'm going to set before you the case for the startling claim Jesus makes—that He is the only way to heaven, that He is the only way to a meaningful life today and eternal life with Him tomorrow. Once you have finished reading, decide for yourself.

1

The Beginning of It All

What is the sum of two plus two?

Four, you say?

What if I told you that two plus two equals five? Would you still insist that the answer is four?

If I choose to believe two plus two equals five, who are you to tell me I'm wrong? Some people might say that two plus two equals three. Others might say that two plus two equals a hundred or a thousand or a gazillion.

You may be thinking, *Two plus two always equals four. It's not a matter of opinion. It's a matter of fact.*

Well, you have *your* truth, but someone else may have a *different* truth. It's fine to say that two plus two equals four. That answer may be the right answer for you, but who's to say it's the right answer for everyone?

Don't all paths ultimately lead to the correct answer?

You aren't suggesting that some people's answers are actually *wrong*, are you? Don't you realize how intolerant and narrow-minded you sound?

THE TRUE MEANING OF TOLERANCE

No one likes to be called intolerant. We prize our reputation for tolerance, just as we prize our reputation for being intelligent, honest, and so forth. We hate to have other people think that we are narrow-minded or bigoted in any way.

Some people may think it's intolerant and narrow-minded to say that two plus two never equals three, never equals five, but only equals four. But if you are not willing to accept the fact that two plus two *always* equals four, then you are going to be at a serious disadvantage in this world. You won't be able to correctly count your change at the grocery store, balance your checkbook, or fill out your tax return—

and that's when you'll find out how intolerant the Internal Revenue Service can be.

We must always be tolerant of other people in terms of differing opinions, ethnicity, language, and so forth. We must always treat other people with respect and learn to get along with them. That kind of tolerance is an admirable quality, and we all need to practice it.

But sometimes people misuse the word "tolerance." For example, there have been times when I have said, "Jesus is the only way to God the Father," and people have said to me, "That's an intolerant statement. That's religious bigotry. You need to be tolerant of other people's beliefs."

Well, I *am* tolerant of other people's beliefs. I have never forced any Muslim or Buddhist or atheist, or person of no religion at all, to accept my beliefs. I am willing to listen to their views, and I don't hesitate to share mine in a polite and respectful way. But I will not say that Islam or Buddhism or atheism is as valid as faith in Jesus Christ, because He says otherwise. The belief that Jesus is the way, the truth, and the life is central to God's truth. The greatest lie says, "No, Jesus is one of many ways that will take you to heaven."

You and I can disagree over our respective beliefs, and I promise I will still treat you cordially. I will not pretend to agree with you. While I have the evidence on my side, I will be respectful. As long as you are cordial and respectful, we will get along just fine in spite of our disagreements. That's what it means to be genuinely tolerant of one another.

IN THE BEGINNING

The real world is not very tolerant of mistaken beliefs. It is easier to believe the greatest lie than to examine the facts.

For example, you may choose to believe that one liquid is pretty much the same as another liquid. But if you fill your car's fuel tank with prune juice instead of gasoline, you'll soon discover that the engine is intolerant of prune juice. And if you fill your juice glass with gasoline and drink it down, you'll quickly discover that your body is intolerant of gasoline.

The world has always been this way, ever since the creation of the human race. In the beginning, God created the human race with a man and a woman named Adam and Eve. God placed the man and the woman in a garden which He prepared for them—the Garden of Eden (Gen. 1 & 2).

If you are a skeptic, you might say, "I don't believe the Bible. I don't believe the story of Adam and Eve." Well, I won't tell you what to believe. I will simply tell you what the historical evidence says, and you are free to draw your own conclusions.

As we go along, I think you will see how the opening chapters of Genesis explain the sufferings and sorrows that have tormented the human race through history, right up to the present day. In the Bible's first few pages, we find the source of our fear of death. We learn why we are plagued by a nagging sense of shame, guilt, and separation from God.

The Genesis story begins with the Creator bringing the universe into existence out of nothing. He placed a formless earth in an empty void and reshaped the planet, dividing the land from the water and the soil from the sky. Our heavenly Father brought forth a myriad of life-forms upon the earth. In the midst of it all, He created a beautiful garden called Eden. There He placed the first man and the first woman—Adam and Eve.

The Bible tells us that God created Adam and Eve to enjoy an intimate relationship with Him. The first humans experienced daily friendship and fellowship with their Creator. They had complete freedom to enjoy all the delights of the garden—except one. God placed a single prohibition on their freedom: "You must not eat from the tree of the knowledge of good and evil, for when you eat of it you will surely die" (Gen. 2:17).

But while God prohibited them from eating of that tree, He also gave them the gift of free will. Adam and Eve were free to obey God—and free to disobey.

At the end of Genesis 2, we find Adam and Eve living an idyllic existence in their garden paradise. But at the beginning of chapter three, Eve encounters the serpent—Satan disguised as one of the creatures in the garden. The serpent asks the woman, "Did God really say, 'You must not eat from any tree in the garden'?"

Eve replies, "We may eat fruit from the trees in the garden, but God did say, 'You must not eat fruit from the tree that is in the middle of the garden, and you must not touch it, or you will die.'"

"You will not surely die," the serpent said. "For God knows that when you eat of it your eyes will be opened, and you will be like God, knowing good and evil" (Gen. 3:1-5).

In other words, Satan told Eve, "Surely, God could not have meant literally that you would die. He would never be so intolerant as to deny you the experience of tasting of that tree. God just told you that because He didn't want you to become as wise as He is."

What does that statement remind you of? To me, it sounds very much like the voices we hear today: "Surely, Jesus could not have meant He is the *only* way to God. He would never be so intolerant. Jesus only said that because He wanted many people to follow Him. He's *a* path to God, but surely there are many *other* paths which ultimately lead to God."

The serpent offered his false "wisdom," which is now the world's "wisdom." Seduced by the serpent's "wisdom," Eve took of the fruit, ate of it, and then gave it to Adam. After Adam and Eve tasted the fruit, they discovered that, just as God had warned, there were consequences for the sin of disobeying His commandment. They fell for the greatest lie—hook, line, and sinker.

Genesis 3:7-10 tells us, "Then the eyes of both of them were opened, and they realized they were naked;

so they sewed fig leaves together and made coverings for themselves. Then the man and his wife heard the sound of the Lord God as he was walking in the garden in the cool of the day, and they hid from the Lord God among the trees of the garden. But the Lord God called to the man, 'Where are you?' He answered, 'I heard you in the garden, and I was afraid because I was naked; so I hid.'"

Adam and Eve enjoyed a trusting friendship with their Creator until they disobeyed His commandment. At that moment, their relationship with Him was broken. For the first time in their lives, they were afraid of God and ashamed in His presence. They covered themselves and hid from His sight.

Falling for the greatest lie leads to disobedience, and disobedience placed a barrier between humanity and God which exists to this day. You and I still live in the tragic aftermath of that wrongful choice.

THE KEY TO OUR HUMANITY

The Genesis story is the story of your origin and mine. It discloses not only what God has done in the past, but what He is doing in our lives today—and what

He will do in the future. We can't understand where we are going unless we know where we have been.

That's why God gave us the first book of the Bible: Genesis. There, you and I learn we are the children of Adam and Eve. The shame, fear, depression, anxiety, and feeling of separation from God that they felt after their disobedience mirrors our feelings when we sin. So you and I can identify with Adam and Eve.

The shadow of sin placed an impassable chasm between our forbearers and their Creator. God exiled Adam and Eve from the garden—sending them out into the wide and hostile world beyond. They were forced to begin a new life in the harsh wilderness outside of paradise. They could see their lost garden home but could no longer live there.

Adam toiled in constant, back-breaking labor against weeds, thorns, and thistles in order to produce just enough food to keep himself and his family alive. His skin grew bronzed and weathered, and his flesh was scarred and seamed due to the thorns of the ground and the attacks of predatory animals.

Eve became pregnant and suffered pain in childbirth—another consequence of sin. The children born to Adam and Eve grew into sinful, rebellious adults. One of their children murdered the other, bringing incredible sorrow into their lives. The years passed—years of sorrow and regret. Adam and Eve grew old and eventually died.

The human race multiplied, and so did the human sin of believing the greatest lie. The gap between humanity and God grew wider and wider. Human beings increasingly rebelled against His laws and commandments. The descendents of Adam and Eve created a civilization opposed to God's rule.

Many people treat the story of Adam and Eve as a quaint fable—yet this story actually contains the key to our humanity. It explains why we are the way we are, both as individuals and as a human community. It reveals both our brilliance and our folly, the splendor of our achievements and the horrors of our crimes. Genesis was written thousands of years ago, and the story of the Garden of Eden has been told and retold countless times. Yet it is still relevant in this and every age.

THE PROMISE OF A SAVIOR

The story of Adam and Eve tells us that we were created in the image of God, created for fellowship with Him, and created for greatness. But by falling for the greatest lie, Adam and Eve broke that fellowship and toppled our race from its unfallen position. That sin produced generation after generation of rebellion, selfishness, and suffering.

You and I were created for the Garden; but the sin of Adam exiled us to the wilderness. The disobedience of the first human beings produced in us a spiritual "genetic disorder." As a result, the sin nature of Adam and Eve has been inherited, generation after generation, by every child of the human race.

Just as sin separated Adam and Eve from their Creator, our sin separates us from God. That separation is the source of our lack of contentment, our feelings of guilt, our sense of meaninglessness, our anxiety and depression, and our fear of death. That chasm between us and God is the reason for the terrible emptiness so many people feel, even those who seemingly "have it all"—wealth, power, possessions, fame, and more.

There is only one way for us to overcome the meaninglessness of our existence: we must discover who God designed us to be. He designed us to live in close, continuous fellowship with Him in the Garden of Eden—but we are separated from Him by our sin, just as Adam and Eve were separated from Him by their sin of believing the greatest lie. That's why this ancient story is still so vitally relevant to our lives today. It is repeated a million times a day: "Jesus is not the only Savior."

Yet, God Himself has bridged the gap between us and Him. He has made it possible for us to return (in a spiritual sense) to the Garden. Many people are surprised to discover that God begins restoring that relationship in those same opening chapters of Genesis. Right there, in the Garden of Eden, God reveals to Adam and Eve that He has a plan of salvation for the human race, and that He is going to send a Savior.

We see this in Genesis 3:15, where God says to the serpent, "And I will put enmity between you and the woman, and between your offspring and hers; he will crush your head, and you will strike his heel." The "offspring" of Eve, of course, is Jesus. In symbolic language, which Adam and Eve could not fully understand, God predicted the coming of Jesus Christ. Satan would strike at Him, tempting Him in the wilderness without success, opposing His ministry through the attacks of the religious leaders, and ultimately nailing Him to a cross. Thus Satan would strike His heel.

But Jesus would rise again on the third day after the crucifixion. The day Jesus walked forth from the tomb; He crushed the head of Satan and destroyed the power of death. Thus, God's prophecy in Genesis 3:15 was fulfilled in the New Testament.

The story of Adam and Eve is told at the beginning of the Bible for an important reason. This account enables us to make sense of who we are as human beings and to understand how we fit into God's plan for human history. The entire Bible, from Genesis to Revelation, is a unified and systematic whole. Its books tower like a brilliantly designed, well-constructed skyscraper—and the entire edifice rests upon the foundation of the story of Adam and Eve.

The Scriptures show us what God did in the past so that we can understand what He is doing in our lives today and what He is going to do in the future. The story of the human race has a beginning, a middle, and an end. It's a story "written" in time and space in the actual events of history. Through this story, the Author of these events makes Himself personally known to us. The better we know Him, the better we understand ourselves.

BETWEEN THE BEGINNING AND THE END

The beginning of humanity's story mirrors the end of our story in Revelation. In Genesis, human beings live in an indescribably beautiful garden—experiencing perfect fellowship and communion with their Creator. In Revelation, resurrected human beings live in a beautiful garden city that comes down from heaven, and they experience the perfect fellowship with God that He intended from the beginning. The loss of innocence in the Garden of Eden is mirrored by the restoration of innocence at the end of time.

The opening chapters of Genesis depict the first wedding—the union between Adam and Eve. Genesis chapter two tells us that God made a woman from a rib taken out of the man, and God brought her to Adam. And Adam said, "This is now bone of my bones and flesh of my flesh; she shall be called 'woman,' for she was taken out of man." And Genesis adds, "For this reason a man will leave his father and mother and be united to his wife, and they will become one flesh" (vv. 23-24).

In a striking parallel, the book of Revelation presents another marriage ceremony. It is the wedding of the Bridegroom (the Lord Jesus Christ) and His bride (believers from every century, every ethnic group, and every nation who refused to believe the greatest lie and accepted God's greatest gift). The writer of Revelation describes a voice like rushing waters and the sound of thunder saying, "Let us rejoice and be glad and give him glory! For the wedding of the Lamb has come, and his bride has made herself ready." Then, he said that an angel told him, "Write: 'Blessed are those who are invited to the wedding supper of the Lamb!'" (Rev. 19:7, 9).

The parallels between the first and last books of the Bible continue: in Genesis, the Creator gives human beings authority over His creation. In Revelation, God's people are given authority to reign over creation with Jesus. Genesis begins with humanity's creation in a place of peace and joy. Revelation ends with redeemed humanity entering into a place of even greater peace and eternal joy. Heaven is described throughout the Old and New Testaments. The prophet Isaiah writes, "'The wolf and the lamb will feed together, and the lion will eat straw like the ox, but dust will be the serpent's food. They will neither harm nor destroy on all my holy mountain,' says the Lord" (Isa. 65:25).

Clearly, something happens between Genesis and Revelation, between the beginning and the end of the human story. Something mysterious takes place to make that mirror-perfect ending possible. The problem of sin is solved. All our guilt, restlessness, fear, depression, self-hate, and despair, which are symptoms of our spiritual "genetic disorder," are healed. The human condition is transformed.

What takes place between Genesis and Revelation to bring about such a transformation in our eternal destiny?

The answer lies ahead.

2

The Big Lie

Who is a true authority on cancer—the cancer patient or the cancer surgeon?

The patient knows cancer in an experiential way. He knows the sensations, the painful and frightening symptoms, the dread, the anxiety, the debilitating effects of the disease.

But the surgeon knows cancer in a clinical way. He has studied the pathology of cancer, its diagnosis, causes, treatment, and prognosis. He has examined cancer cells under a microscope, identified tumors in x-rays, and surgically removed cancerous growths from human bodies.

Both the patient and surgeon know cancer well. But they know the disease differently. The knowledge of the patient and the knowledge of the surgeon are different kinds of knowledge. The experience of the patient and the experience of the surgeon are as different as night and day.

The patient as a sufferer. The surgeon as a true authority.

In the Garden of Eden, Satan (in the guise of a serpent) came to Eve with the Big Lie. He told her that she could become a true authority on good and evil. He told her, in effect, that if she would choose to disobey God and fall for the Big Lie, she could become the spiritual equivalent of a surgeon, having a complete and authoritative knowledge of this spiritual "cancer" called sin.

Eve believed the Big Lie. In so doing, she became not an authority on sin, but a sufferer of sin.

In the previous chapter we saw the serpent ask Eve, "Did God really say, 'You must not eat from any tree in the garden'?"

She replied, "We may eat fruit from the trees in the garden, but God did say, 'You must not eat fruit from the tree that is in the middle of the garden, *and you must not touch it*, or you will die.'" (Note the italicized phrase.)

At that point, Satan knew that Eve was ready to believe the Big Lie and would fall for the greatest lie. How did Satan know this? Because Eve twisted her Creator's command. In Genesis 2:16-17, God told Adam, "You are free to eat from any tree in the garden; but you must not eat from the tree." But Eve added something to that command which her Creator did not say, ". . . and you must not touch it."

Perhaps she had already begun to question God's command. Every tree in the garden was hers to enjoy except one—yet it seems her attention was focused on that one forbidden tree. Perhaps Satan had watched the woman as she walked around the tree, studying it from every angle. Perhaps he saw a gleam of curiosity in her eyes. Eve was fascinated by the tree—and Satan knew her area of weakness and how best to attack it.

So Satan hit her with his best lie—the Big Lie. He said to her, "You will not surely die. For God knows that when you eat of it your eyes will be opened, and you will be like God, knowing good and evil."

In other words, "If you eat of the tree, you will become wise, an authority on good and evil. Your understanding will be as great as God's own understanding." Satan promised Eve that she would have knowledge of good and evil—and his promise was half-true. By disobeying God, she would indeed experience sin. By being infected by sin, she would suffer from it and come to know the difference between good and evil—in the most horrible way imaginable.

But Satan also promised that this experiential knowledge of sin would make her like God, with a divine understanding of good and evil. That was a complete lie. Satan still offers us the same Big Lie today, and we continue to fall for it. Pride, which is another way of falling into the greatest lie, keeps many people from accepting God's plan of salvation. Make sure you are not one of them.

STILL FALLING FOR THE OLDEST LIE IN THE BOOK

When Eve took the fruit and ate of it, she instantly knew the difference between good and evil—because she had just committed an evil act. She had crossed the line from obedience to disobedience—and from innocence to guilt.

Her next act was to offer the fruit to her husband. Why did she do this? Eve had already condemned herself. Why did she invite Adam to join her? Perhaps in her selfishness, Eve didn't want to be alone. Misery loves company, and so does sin. Knowing she had done wrong and knowing she had crossed the line from life to death, Eve didn't want to be alone. So she offered the fruit to Adam and invited him to eat.

He ate—and at that moment, Adam knew good from evil. Having tasted evil of his own free will, he lost the good.

So Adam and Eve fell—and we fell with them. As a result, the entire human race has come to know sin and evil in an experiential way. None of us is an *authority* on sin. We are all *sufferers* of the sin disease.

Again, if you are a skeptic, you may say, "But I don't believe in magical fruit growing on magical trees, which magically gives people the knowledge of good and evil. That's just a fairy tale for primitive people and children." Again, I'm not going to tell you what to believe. I'm simply going to let the Bible speak for itself. You are free to draw your own conclusions.

But I will say this: the Bible does not tell us that there was any "magic" in the fruit. There is nothing in the Genesis story which suggests that any specific properties of the fruit caused Eve to suddenly become aware of the difference between good and evil.

It was the *act of disobedience itself that* opened her eyes to the reality of good and evil. It is by choosing to disobey God's command that she entered into the experience of sin. In the moment she chose disobedience, a profound change took place within Eve's mind, heart, and spirit: she ceased to believe in God as God and accept His word as the final authority.

The moment Eve made her choice, she stopped believing in Him as her all-wise Creator and Friend. Instead, she convinced herself that God was preventing her from experiencing the goodness of the tree and the godlike knowledge of good and evil. She doubted that the Creator truly wanted the best for her. In fact, she actually believed Satan's suggestion that God had *lied* to her.

That is the devil's Big Lie.

Doesn't it sound familiar? If you believe in God, you have probably experienced times of doubt and questioning. You've wondered if He is really wise and perfect, if He really wants the best for you, if He really loves you, or if His commands are truly good and worthy of your obedience. You may have questioned whether God is even telling you the truth, or whether He really is God.

Perhaps you wondered if His commands are meant only to restrict you and ruin your enjoyment of life. Maybe He doesn't really understand you at all. Jesus said He is the way and the truth and the life—the only path to God the Father. But what if *that* is a lie? What if there *are* many paths to God? What if there is no heaven, no hell, but we are simply reincarnated and keep coming back to live a succession of lives—the quality of which depends on the karma we accumulate?

Such questions tempt, intoxicate, and lure us. These suggestions and questions ultimately come to us from one source: the serpent in the Garden, Satan himself. The lie of "many paths to God" suggests to us, "A God of love would allow people to come to Him by any road they choose—through living a good life, through the teachings of Buddha or Mohammed, or through meditation and reincarnation. I prefer to believe that everyone is going to heaven whether they believe in Jesus or not."

Some of the best-selling books of our age preach and teach the Big Lie. One best-selling author describes Jesus as "a savior. Not *the* savior, not the one and only

Son of God. Rather, Jesus embodied the highest level of enlightenment. He spent his brief adult life describing it, teaching it, and passing it on to future generations. *Jesus intended to save the world by showing others the path to God-consciousness*" (italics in the original).[1]

Notice the sentence in italics. Not only does this author tell us that Jesus is merely *a* savior among many (and thus just one path among many to God). This author actually preaches that Jesus came *not* to save the world from sin but to point the way to "God-consciousness." In other words, this author claims that Jesus' message was the same message Satan gave to Eve: "Your eyes will be opened, and you will be like God."

Has there ever been a bigger lie than *this* Big Lie? Has there ever been another lie that people were so eager to buy and wallow in? The author who wrote the words I just quoted has sold millions of books, appeared on numerous TV shows, and been praised by world leaders. So the Big Lie is very popular in our culture today.

Books with titles such as *The Third Jesus*, *A Return to Love*, *A Course in Miracles*, *The Power of Now*, *A New Earth*, and *The Secret* all proclaim the Big Lie that human beings can become like God and enjoy limitless health, wealth, love, sex, and eternal youth. All of these books sell millions of copies, which is proof that people still fall for the oldest lie in the Book.

Isn't it amazing? The people who buy these books think they are hearing the latest "truths." Yet it's all the same Big Lie which Satan used to entice Eve in the Garden: "You can have everything you want by following *your* way or somebody else's way instead of God's way."

The Still, Small Voice

Adam and Eve were created with the freedom to choose God's way or the Big Lie. They chose the lie.

From the moment our original ancestors made that fateful decision, our own genetic code has been tainted by the moral and spiritual virus of naked self-will, of wanting to believe the greatest deception, and of rebelling against God's plan for our lives. Centuries have come and gone since the fall of humanity, and we still believe that lie.

Bowing to alternative views that appeal to us has always been a temptation. We refuse to believe there is only one way of salvation, only one way to the Father. We choose to believe there are many paths to God.

Why? Because if there are many paths to God instead of just one, then we can willfully and selfishly choose the path *we* want. We can live the way *we* want, and never be held accountable by God. We can choose a religion that appeals to our own pride and vanity.

The Big Lie of Satan is so appealing to human nature that we actually hear this line being offered from some church pulpits and religious TV programs. Many preachers, ambitious for wealth and fame and a mass audience, have modified the Lord's claim that He is the only way to the Father. It doesn't matter how large a following a preacher has or how many books he has sold—if he tells you there is any path to God other than Jesus Himself, then he is selling the same Big Lie which seduced Adam and Eve.

The Big Lie of Satan destroyed humanity's fellowship with God in the Garden of Eden. It continues to destroy human lives to this day. But you don't have to be deceived by the Lie. You can know the truth, and God's truth *will* set you free (John 8:32).

Adam and Eve once lived within the safe and protective enclosure of the Garden, walking and talking with their Creator, enjoying fellowship with Him. That is the life God intended for us all—and He still wants you to experience that way of life today. He wants friendship and fellowship with you. He wants to listen to your thoughts and feelings, your wants and needs, your hopes and dreams. Most important of all, He is eager to talk to you and guide you—if you will listen.

There is an account in the Old Testament in which the prophet Elijah went up on a mountaintop to hear the voice of God. As Elijah stood upon the mountain, a great wind whipped up, breaking the rocks in pieces, causing an avalanche. But the Lord was not in the wind. Next, a great earthquake shook the mountain to its foundation. But the Lord was not in the earthquake. After the earthquake came a blast of fire. But the Lord was not in the fire.

After the fire came "a gentle whisper"—a still, small voice. That gentle whisper, that still, small voice, was the voice Elijah heard (1 Kings 19:11-13). It was the voice of God's own Spirit. It is the same voice that you and I can hear if we take the time to quiet our thoughts. It is my prayer that you would hear His voice through the pages of this book.

3

The Tale of Three Gardens

We find three different gardens occurring at three crucial moments in the biblical story of humanity—at the beginning, the middle, and the end. The first garden is the Garden of Eden. That garden was a place of peace and protection where Adam and Eve received the gift of life, came together in marriage, and experienced intimate fellowship with God.

The second garden—well, we'll cover that in just a moment.

We find the third garden in the center of the New Jerusalem. In the book of Revelation, John describes a scene from his vision of heaven: "Then the angel showed me the river of the water of life, as clear as crystal, flowing from the throne of God and of the Lamb down the middle of the great street of the city. On each side of the river stood the tree of life, bearing twelve crops of fruit, yielding its fruit every month. And the leaves of the tree are for the healing of the nations. No longer will there be any curse . . ." (Rev. 22:1-3).

The fruit of that one tree in the first garden—the Garden of Eden—inflicted the curse of death on the human race. The tree in the third garden—the tree of life beside the river of life—yields a continuous harvest of life-giving fruit. The leaves of the tree are for the healing of nations. And the curse of death shall finally come to an end.

Clearly, something must have happened between the first garden and the third garden to bring about such a dramatic transformation. Some event must have taken place between Genesis and Revelation to completely alter the fate of humanity and lift that curse.

That event, of course, took place in the second garden—the garden we find in the middle of humanity's story. That second garden was the Garden of Gethsemane—the garden outside the walls of Jerusalem. There Jesus struggled in prayer the night before He was crucified.

In the first garden, human beings were tempted by Satan to eat the forbidden fruit. In the second garden, Jesus—whom Paul called "the last Adam" or "the second Adam" (1 Cor. 15:45-49)—faced a far more intense temptation. The first Adam was simply commanded not to eat the fruit of one tree. But the last Adam, Jesus, was being sent to an agonizing death upon another "tree," the cross of Calvary.

In that second garden, the perfect Son of God was tempted to reject God's plan for the human race, the agony of the cross, and temporary but total separation from God the Father. The temptation Jesus faced was so excruciating that the act of prayer itself became an agony. Sweat poured from his brow like drops of blood (Luke 22:44).

There in the Garden of Gethsemane, Jesus battled Satan through absolute reliance upon the power of God the Father. He drew upon the same Source of strength that is available to you and me for rejecting the greatest lie. In that garden, Jesus settled the matter when He said, "Not My will, but Yours be done" (v. 42).

He chose obedience—submitting Himself to the Father's will and surrendering His life on the cross. His obedient submission guaranteed the Enemy's defeat. There, Jesus crushed the head of the serpent, fulfilling God's promise in Genesis 3:15.

In the first garden, Adam and Eve yielded to Satan, believed his greatest lie, ate the forbidden fruit, and, by their disobedience, infected all of their physical descendents with the virus of sin. In the second garden, Jesus submitted to God the Father, drank the cup of judgment for us all, and by His obedience enabled His spiritual descendents to be healed of the deadly "sin virus."

As members of Adam's race, we are infected with the "virus" of sin. But we can be healed when we respond to Jesus and receive the gift of forgiveness and eternal life which He offers us. The gift is free, but you must be willing to accept it. Once you do, you will be raised to life by the power of the One who has defeated Satan and overcome death.

It's your choice. As long as you choose to live apart from God the Father and His Son Jesus, you will be helpless in the grip of guilt and fear. You will remain outside of the Garden, exiled in the wilderness.

WHAT ABOUT HELL?

If you accept the notion that all paths lead to God, then logically you must also believe that there are no paths which lead to hell. If all paths lead to God, then hell is either empty or does not exist. The problem with this view is that hell is spoken of repeatedly in the Scriptures. In fact, most of what we know about hell is revealed by Jesus Himself.

Several times in the Bible, Jesus described hell as a literal place of eternal punishment and torment (Mark 9:43-44; Matt. 10:28; 13:40-42; 18:8-10; 25:46; Luke 16:22-31). Hell was designed as a place of punishment for Satan and the fallen angels (Matt. 25:41; Rev. 20:10), but it will also be a place of punishment for those who reject God's gift of salvation through Jesus Christ (Rev. 20:12-15).

You may choose to believe that all paths lead to God, but Jesus Himself clearly taught that all other paths lead to eternal torment in hell. He spent a great deal of time warning against hell and describing that place in graphic detail.

People have asked, "How dare you say that a Buddhist or a Muslim or a sincere atheist cannot go to heaven, simply because he doesn't agree with your religious views?"

Often I reply, "No one will ever go to hell because they disagree with me. My opinions are of no importance. But I fear for those who fall for the greatest lie and reject God's only plan for salvation. I fear for those who refuse to see the sacrifice of Christ as the only way. I fear for those who reject the grace of God."

If you are in a place where they tell you that hell is merely a metaphor, then I suggest you leave as quickly as possible. You will not find God's truth there.

You might ask, "How could a loving God send anyone to hell?" The answer might surprise you: God never sends anyone to hell. All of those who end up in that place of eternal torment—whether human beings or Satan and his demons—have placed themselves there by their own choice. They have refused to accept that it is the grace of God alone that can save.

At a great cost to Himself, our loving Father has made it possible for *everyone* to receive eternal life in heaven with Him. He sent His only Son to suffer and die on the cross so we would not have to endure the punishment of hell. The New Testament tells us, "The Lord . . . is patient with you, not wanting anyone to perish, but everyone to come to repentance" (2 Peter 3:9). Clearly, God has no desire to send anyone to hell, but He will not overrule our own free will. If we choose an eternity in hell, He will not send us to heaven against our will.

You might ask, "But what about those who have never heard the good news of Jesus Christ?" People have asked me that question hundreds of times. Here is my answer: don't worry about those who haven't heard. They are God's responsibility, not yours. What is your responsibility? Simply this: once you have heard the good news of Jesus Christ, you must make a decision. What will your decision be? Will you accept the grace that God offers you through His Son? Or will you reject it?

"But, what evidence do I have that the gospel is the truth—and that Jesus Himself is the way to eternal life?" you ask.

If it's evidence you want—proof of the claims of Jesus Christ—then turn the page with me. And prepare to be amazed.

4

The Indisputable Truth

Why should you believe in Jesus as the only Savior and Lord?

Why should His claim to be the way, the truth, and the life be taken seriously? Anyone can say, "Follow me. I am the only way to God." Why should we believe the claims of Jesus Christ over those of anyone else?

Answer: only Jesus supported His claim with indisputable evidence.

In fact, there is a *mountain* of evidence to support His claim—enough to fill many books. But let me just cite a few examples—historical proof that Jesus truly was (as God promised in Genesis 3:15) the One who would come to save Adam and his descendents from their sins.

Let's start at the beginning of the story of Jesus—His birth. For centuries, believers have treasured the Christmas story, while skeptics have doubted and dismissed it as a religious myth. But recent advances in astronomy, computer science, and history have given us a powerful confirmation of the biblical account of the birth of Jesus Christ.

The Christmas account in Matthew 2:1-12 tells us that "Magi from the east" came to Jerusalem asking, "Where is the one who has been born king of the Jews? We saw his star in the east and have come to worship him." The Magi were wise and learned men, royal astronomers from the region of Persia. These highly educated astronomers were familiar with the Jewish Scriptures, which predicted the coming Messiah. The Magi had seen an unusual event among the stars, and they believed that this event announced the birth of a new King of the Jews.

The gospel of Matthew explains how King Herod became quite disturbed when he heard that these Persian astronomers were in Jerusalem searching for a newborn "King of the Jews." After all, Herod was the reigning king of the Jews, even though he was little more than a puppet of the Roman Empire.

A worried and agitated Herod called his advisors together, and asked them where (according to Old Testament prophecy) the Messiah was to be born. His advisors quoted Micah 5:2, which predicted that the Messiah would be born in the town of Bethlehem. So King Herod called the Magi to his palace and sent them to Bethlehem to find the child. Though Herod told the Magi he wanted to worship the newborn King, he actually wanted to kill the child because he feared that this newborn King threatened his reign.

ANCIENT PROPHECY AND TWENTY-FIRST-CENTURY SCIENCE

The Magi set off for Bethlehem, a town about five miles south of Jerusalem. As they approached the town, the Persian astronomers saw the star—the very same star they had seen rising in the east—shining over Bethlehem. When they arrived there, the Magi found Mary with the child Jesus. They presented Him with expensive gifts and worshiped Him. Later, because of a warning they received in a dream, they returned back to their own land without reporting to King Herod.

For centuries, many people have interpreted this story as suggesting that the star of Bethlehem moved around in the sky, guiding the Magi from place to place until it finally led them to Bethlehem. After all, the book of Matthew tells us that the star "went ahead of them until it stopped over the place where the child was" (2:9). Various phenomena have been suggested to explain the star of Bethlehem: a meteor, a comet, or an exploding star in the sky. But none of these fit the description in Matthew or any known astronomical events in history.

Then along came an American attorney, Frederick A. Larson. He has a B.A. degree in Philosophy and a Juris Doctor degree from the University of Southern California. Larson has worked as an attorney, a prosecutor, and a judge, so he knows how to investigate facts, evaluate evidence, and arrive at the truth of a matter.

After carefully studying Matthew's account of the Christmas story, Larson used a home computer and sophisticated astronomy software to map the skies over Jerusalem in the years 2 and 3 BC. In the process, he made an amazing discovery: the facts surrounding the star of Bethlehem in Matthew's account seemed to fit the behavior and appearance of the planet Jupiter as it passed through the night skies in 3 BC.

Planets, in Matthew's time, were known as "wandering stars," because in their motion around the sun they moved against the background of all the other fixed stars in the universe. And Jupiter, the largest of all the planets, has been known since ancient times as the king of the wandering stars. The motion of Jupiter brought it in close proximity with the star Regulus in September of 3 BC—right at the time of Rosh Hashanah, the Jewish New Year. The Romans, Babylonians, and other people of that time all regarded Regulus as "the king star." Larson surmised that when the "king planet" appeared to touch the "king star" at the time of the Jewish new year, the Magi took note. They believed it to be a sign announcing the birth of the King of the Jews.

There is far more detail to Larson's explanation than I can go into here. All of it is fascinating and convincing, and I encourage you to view the DVD he produced entitled *The Star of Bethlehem*. Larson explains that, according to the computer-generated sky maps of that era, Jupiter would be visible in the vicinity of Regulus from September of 3 BC through June of 2 BC as the Magi journeyed toward Jerusalem.[1] Traveling at night to avoid the heat of the day, the Magi would have been able to follow the "star," which rose in the east and set in the west, as they headed westward toward Jerusalem.

After meeting with King Herod in Jerusalem, the Magi traveled a short distance south to Bethlehem. "To qualify as the star," Larson says, "Jupiter would have to have been ahead of the Magi as they trekked south from Jerusalem to Bethlehem." According to the computer-generated sky maps of that time, Larson concludes, "In December of 2 BC., if the Magi looked south in the wee hours, there hung the Planet of Kings over the city of [the] Messiah's birth."[1]

Larson reminds us that Matthew 2:9 mentions a specific behavior of the star of Bethlehem: "The star they had seen in the east went ahead of them until it stopped over the place where the child was." The star *stopped*? If the star of Bethlehem was Jupiter, how could that star stop over the town of Bethlehem? Again, Matthew's account is confirmed by scientific evidence.

According to the computer-generated star maps, Jupiter, the "king planet," experienced a period of what astronomers call "retrograde motion." Though the planet was actually moving in orbit around the sun, Jupiter appears to stop in its tracks as viewed from planet earth. That is, it appears to come to a dead stop relative to the background stars—then it appears to move once again. The Magi would have noticed when Jupiter appeared to come to a complete halt in the sky.

The sky maps show that Jupiter appeared to stop on December 25 of the year 2 BC, the very night of the year that we celebrate as Christmas, the birthday of Jesus Christ. Isn't that amazing? Matthew's account of the birth of Jesus combines with twenty-first-century science to affirm that Jesus is truly the Messiah—the Savior promised by God in Genesis 3:15.

"My Time Has Not Yet Come."

Jesus was born in Bethlehem, grew up in Nazareth, and performed his first miracle in the Galilean town of Cana. John 2:1-11 tells of the time Jesus attended a wedding and the bridegroom ran out of wine.

Mary, the mother of Jesus, asked Him to perform a spectacular miracle that would make Him famous throughout the region. Jesus replied, "Dear woman, why do you involve me in this problem? My time has not yet come."

Then, instead of creating a sensation by performing a miracle in front of the entire crowd, He quietly turned water into wine. He didn't call attention to Himself, and the only ones who knew about the miracle were His disciples and the servants who served the wine. Jesus was not ready to announce Himself as King and Messiah. His time had not yet come.

Sometime after performing this first miracle, Jesus' brothers said to Him, "You ought to leave here and go to Judea, so that your disciples may see the miracles you do. No one who wants to become a public figure acts in secret. Since you are doing these things, show yourself to the world" (John 7:3-4). They were goading Him and making fun of Him because they didn't believe He was the Messiah.

Jesus replied that He wasn't seeking publicity— not yet. "The right time for me has not yet come," He said (v. 6).

Several times throughout His ministry, Jesus referred to the fact that His life was on a secret timetable. On one occasion, He was walking with His disciples on the road to the town of Caesarea Philippi. As they walked, Jesus asked, "Who do people say the Son of Man is?" The disciples replied that people thought Jesus was John the Baptist or Elijah or Jeremiah or one of the prophets.

Then Jesus turned to Peter and said, "Who do *you* say I am?" And Peter replied, "You are the Christ, the Son of the living God." Jesus blessed Peter because God had revealed this truth to him—but then He added that the disciples should tell no one about this. (See Matthew 16:13-20.) Why did Jesus tell them to keep His identity a secret? Because His time had not yet come.

Finally, after three years of teaching, healing, and raising the dead, Jesus approached the end of His earthly ministry. On the Sunday before He was crucified, the Messiah came into Jerusalem riding on a donkey. Throngs of people who had heard Jesus preach and watched Him perform miracles lined the road, spreading palm branches in His path and shouting, "Blessed is the king who comes in the name of the Lord!" (Luke 19:38).

Enemies of Jesus were also in the crowd, and they shouted to Him, "Teacher, rebuke your disciples!" (v. 39). But Jesus would not silence His followers. Instead, he replied, "If they keep quiet, the stones will cry out" (v. 40).

Again and again throughout His ministry, Jesus instructed the disciples not to tell anyone about His miracles or that He is the Messiah because His time had not yet come. But days before He was to be crucified, Jesus finally permitted His followers to announce Him as the promised King and Messiah. On that day, he openly accepted the praise of the people.

What had changed? Simply this: His time had finally come.

RIGHT ON SCHEDULE

Jesus knew His time had come because He knew the Old Testament prophecies. As He once said to the religious leaders who opposed Him, "You search the Scriptures because you think they give you eternal life. But the Scriptures point to me!" (John 5:39, New

Living Translation). That is a bold claim: all of the Old Testament prophecies point to Jesus alone.

One of the most startling of the Old Testament prophecies is found in Daniel 9:25, "Know and understand this: From the issuing of the decree to restore and rebuild Jerusalem until the Anointed One, the ruler, comes, there will be seven 'sevens,' and sixty-two 'sevens.'" These are the words spoken by the angel Gabriel to Daniel while the Jewish people were held captive in Babylon. These words were recorded centuries before Jesus was born. What do they mean?

The angel Gabriel set forth a precise timetable prophesying when the Messiah—"the Anointed One, the ruler"—would come and be publicly announced before all the people: "There will be seven 'sevens,' and sixty-two 'sevens.'" In other words, the decree to rebuild Jerusalem would be issued, and then there would be seven "sevens" of years plus sixty-two "sevens" of years, at which time the Messiah, the Anointed One, would appear.

Let's do the math. Seven times seven years equals 49 years. Sixty-two times seven years equals 434 years. Add 49 to 434 and you get 483. In those days, the Jewish and Babylonian people used a 360-

day calendar. So, multiply 483 years by 360 days and you get a total of 173,880 days—the span of time from the decree to rebuild Jerusalem until the triumphant appearance of the promised Messiah.

Now here is the truly amazing part. History has recorded the exact day that Artaxerxes I of Persia issued the decree which ordered the reconstruction of Jerusalem. It was March 14, 445 BC. We know this date with such precision because we can compare the biblical record of this decree in Nehemiah 2 with the historical records of King Artaxerxes' reign. If you count 173,880 days from March 14, 445 BC, you arrive at Sunday, April 6, AD 32. By comparing the biblical record with the historical record, we learn that Jesus made his triumphant entry into Jerusalem on the Sunday before the fourth Passover after the fifteenth year of the reign of Tiberius Caesar—which is Sunday, April 6, AD 32.

So, on the exact date the angel Gabriel told Daniel the Messiah would appear, Jesus entered Jerusalem riding on a donkey, exactly as the Old Testament had prophesied. The arrival of the Messiah took place right on schedule—to the exact day.

After 483 years of waiting, His time had finally come.

Bible scholars estimate there are at least 300 prophecies which predict the coming of the Messiah. Those prophecies are scattered throughout the Old Testament, from Genesis to Malachi. They predict His birth, His ministry, His suffering, His death, and His resurrection. As Jesus told His enemies, all of those prophecies point directly to Him.

You may ask, "If the Old Testament pointed so clearly to Jesus as the Lord and Savior of humanity, then why didn't the people of His time remember those prophecies and honor Him as their King?" The answer is simple: prophecies are much easier to understand with the benefit of hindsight. Until they are fulfilled, prophecies seem mysterious and difficult to understand.

The great seventeenth-century English astronomer and mathematician Sir Isaac Newton explained why: "God gave the prophecies, not to gratify men's curiosity by enabling them to foreknow things, but so that after they were fulfilled, they might be interpreted by the event, and God's own providence, not the interpreter's, be thereby manifested to the world."

THE EMPTY TOMB

We already have looked at a number of convincing proofs relating to the claims of Jesus. But let's not forget the most irrefutable proof of all: His resurrection. The tomb of Buddha is occupied. The tomb of Mohammad is occupied. But the tomb of Jesus is empty.

The story of the resurrection of Jesus Christ is told not only in the New Testament, but also in secular accounts. For example, the Jewish historian Josephus wrote in his *Antiquities* (Book 18, Chapter 3):

At this time there was a wise man who was called Jesus. And his conduct was good, and [he] was known to be virtuous. And many people from among the Jews and the other nations became his disciples. Pilate condemned him to be crucified and to die. And those who had become his disciples did not abandon his discipleship. They reported that he had appeared to them three days after his crucifixion and that he was alive; accordingly, he was perhaps the Messiah, concerning whom the prophets have recounted wonders.[2]

The Roman historian Tacitus wrote in Book XV of his *Annals* that Emperor Nero blamed the great fire of Rome on the followers of Jesus:

> Nero fastened the guilt and inflicted the most exquisite tortures on a class hated for their abominations, called Christians by the populace. Christus [Jesus Christ], from whom the name had its origin, suffered the extreme penalty [of death by crucifixion] during the reign of Tiberius at the hands of one of our procurators, Pontius Pilatus, and a most mischievous superstition [belief in the resurrection of Jesus] . . . broke out not only in Judaea, the first source of the evil, but even in Rome, where all things hideous and shameful from every part of the world find their center and become popular.[3]

A skeptic might say, "What does that prove? So Matthew, Mark, Luke, and John reported the story of the resurrection, and two secular historians also referred to the resurrection. But what proof do we have that Jesus actually rose from the dead and walked out of that tomb?"

Actually, we have quite a bit of evidence. Christianity began in Jerusalem, the city where Jesus was crucified and buried. His tomb belonged to Joseph of Arimathea, a prominent man in that community. If you were a citizen of Jerusalem, you could simply take a short walk outside the city walls and inspect the tomb for yourself. Undoubtedly, many citizens of Jerusalem did just that. They visited the tomb, saw that it was empty, and believed in the resurrected Lord. That is undoubtedly one reason why the early church in Jerusalem grew so quickly.

From Jerusalem, the Christian faith spread quickly throughout Judea and outward into Asia Minor, Greece, Italy, Spain, down into North Africa, and eastward to India.

Christianity grew quickly in large part because the resurrection of Jesus was a validated fact. There were hundreds of eyewitnesses who saw and heard the Messiah after He rose from the dead. In fact, the apostle Paul mentions one occurrence where the resurrected Jesus appeared to more than 500 eyewitnesses at one time, most of whom were still living when Paul wrote his letter (1 Cor. 15:6).

The early Christians faced opposition, persecution, and the most horrible forms of torture imaginable, yet they refused to renounce their faith in Jesus Christ. In fact, as persecution grew more intense, the early Christians became bolder and more courageous. Some believers in Jesus were crucified or thrown into arenas to be killed by wild animals. Others were burned alive like torches to light up the palace gardens of Emperor Nero. Would those early Christians endure such torture if they weren't absolutely convinced of the reality of the resurrection?

The evidence is clear and convincing. Jesus is the Savior and Messiah who was promised throughout the Old Testament. He alone fits the precise timetable laid out in Scripture. He lived an extraordinary life. And when it came time for Him to die, He struggled in prayer in the Garden of Gethsemane. He obediently submitted Himself to the will of God the Father, and He died on the cross at Calvary.

But the story does not end there. Jesus rose again. He conquered death. And because He was victorious over the tomb, you and I do not have to fear death. Jesus truly is the way, the truth, and the life. Of that we can be sure.

As we have seen, the first Adam tasted the fruit of the forbidden tree and the result was death. But Jesus, the "second Adam," willingly let Himself be nailed to a tree in obedience to the will of God—then He rose again to give eternal life to everyone who submits to Him as Savior and Lord. If we accept the gift He gives us, we will receive life—abundant life and eternal life, both now and forevermore.

But how do we receive the gift of eternal life? What do we have to do? Read on. These next few chapters could transform you for eternity.

5

The Temporary Solution

Animal sacrifice—the ritual, religious killing of an innocent animal—has been practiced in almost every culture throughout history, from the ancient Hebrews to the Greeks and Romans of ancient Europe to the Hindus of ancient Asia to the Mayans, Aztecs, and Incas of the ancient Americas. There seems to be an instinctive awareness in the human psyche that human sin demands a sacrifice.

In the first book of the Bible, we discover how that awareness came to be implanted within the human soul. In Genesis 3, after Adam and Eve introduced sin into the world, we read: "The Lord God made garments of skin for Adam and his wife and clothed them" (v. 21).

This was the very first instance of animal sacrifice in the history of the human race.

The significance of the garments of skin is twofold. First, the animal skins covered the nakedness of Adam and Eve. After the first humans ate the forbidden fruit, Genesis 3:7 tells us, "Then the eyes of both of them were opened, and they realized they were naked; so they sewed fig leaves together and made coverings for themselves."

Before they sinned, nakedness had never been a cause for shame. But once Adam and Eve crossed over into disobedience and sin, they realized their nakedness. They could not hide their sin. They tried to hide it by covering their bodies with fig leaves sewn together, but their attempt was hopelessly inadequate. God had to provide a covering for the nakedness and shame of their sin—and ours.

Second, the death of the innocent animal was a symbol. It pointed forward to the day when the innocent Lamb of God, Jesus Himself, would be sacrificed upon a cross. The slaughter of the animal was a visual lesson to Adam and Eve of what God would have to do in order to save them and their descendents from the curse of sin.

The book of Genesis does not tell us what kind of animal God killed in order to make garments for Adam and Eve to wear. I suspect that it was a lamb— the fleecy white symbol of gentleness and innocence. Throughout the Old and New Testaments, the lamb symbolizes Jesus Christ as the sacrifice for our sins.

So I think it is likely that, in the presence of Adam and Eve, God slaughtered an innocent lamb for their sakes. He made them watch the sacrifice of innocence. It was the first time they had ever witnessed death. By killing the lamb before their eyes, God set before them a symbol of what it would cost to rescue humanity from the deadly curse of disobedience.

That first sacrifice was a *picture* of the coming Deliverer, the promised Savior who would come in perfect innocence and be slain in full view of a watching humanity. But the sacrifice of the innocent lamb was only a *temporary* solution to the sin problem. It pointed ahead to the *perfect* and *permanent* solution which would take place centuries later—the sacrifice of the Lamb of God upon a wooden cross just outside Jerusalem.

Though the blood of an innocent animal is a startling symbol, it is powerless to save anyone from sin. Only the blood of the sinless Son of God can rescue us and bring forgiveness and salvation to Adam's descendants.

THE TRAGEDY OF CAIN

Adam and Eve understood that the death of the animal symbolized God's promise of a coming Deliverer. From that day forward, the entire human race looked forward to the arrival of the Savior. In fact, when Eve gave birth to her first child in Genesis 4, she named him Cain, a word which in Hebrew suggests "he is brought forth" or "he is here."

This name suggests that Eve mistakenly believed that Cain was the Savior whom God had promised, the Deliverer who would crush the serpent's head and erase the curse of sin. Eventually, it became clear to Adam and Eve that Cain was not the promised Deliverer. In fact, he grew to become a self-willed and rebellious young man.

Cain grew up outside of Eden, having never known the paradise that his parents lost. He never experienced the close fellowship his parents once had with God. Adam and Eve tried to teach Cain right from wrong, but he was spiritually dull. Their teaching could not penetrate his self-centered will. He grew up to become even more disobedient than his parents.

The story of Cain is the story of the first murder. Cain planted crops, while his younger brother Abel was a shepherd. Adam and Eve taught their sons the importance of making sacrifices to the Lord. Cain brought a portion of his crops as a sacrifice, while Abel brought the firstborn sheep of his flock. God accepted Abel's sacrifice of the lambs because it conformed to the first sacrifice witnessed by Adam and Eve. Only the death of an innocent lamb symbolized the death of the coming Messiah.

By offering the Lord grain from the soil, Cain showed that he missed the point of the sacrifice. Perhaps if Cain's heart had been right with God, he would have known why his sacrifice was unacceptable. But Cain was rebellious and angry. God urged him to change his attitude and make his heart right.

God said, "Why are you angry? Why is your face downcast? If you do what is right, will you not be accepted? But if you do not do what is right, sin is crouching at your door; it desires to have you, but you must master it" (vv. 6-7).

Cain refused to listen to God's gracious pleadings. Instead, he lured his brother Abel into a field. There he attacked his brother and killed him.

When God came to Cain and asked him where Abel was, Cain lied: "'I don't know,' he replied. 'Am I my brother's keeper?'" (v. 9). His answer dripped with resentment and sarcasm.

God's response was immediate and absolute: "The LORD said, 'What have you done? Listen! Your brother's blood cries out to me from the ground. Now you are under a curse and driven from the ground, which opened its mouth to receive your brother's blood from your hand. When you work the ground, it will no longer yield its crops for you. You will be a restless wanderer on the earth'" (vv. 10-12). God exiled Cain for murdering his brother, just as He exiled Cain's parents for their sin.

THE BEGINNING OF HORRORS AND SORROWS

Some people wonder why God punished Adam and Eve so severely for violating a command which seems (from a human perspective) seemingly minor: "You must not eat from the tree of the knowledge of good and evil" (Gen. 2:17). Some would say, "Why was God so mean to Adam and Eve? All they did was pick some fruit off a tree and eat it. It's not as if they *killed* anybody."

But notice what a short distance it was from the sin of eating the forbidden fruit to the sin of murder. What a shock and a sorrow it must have been for Eve. At Cain's birth, she had hoped that her firstborn son would grow up to become the promised Savior and Deliverer. Instead, he became the first murderer, taking the life of her second-born son and doubling her grief.

How Adam and Eve must have blamed themselves for willfully defying the Creator! From that one act of sin flowed more horror and suffering than they ever imagined possible: one son slain, the other exiled. And that was only the beginning of the sorrows to come.

CENTURIES OF PROPHECY FULFILLED

Adam and Eve had more children, and their children had children. The years went by. Generation after generation watched and waited for the coming Deliverer whom God had promised. The Old Testament sacrifices were vivid reminders that a Savior was coming. The human race suffered through century after century—the time of Noah, the time of Abraham, the time of Jacob, the time of Moses. God raised up prophets in Israel, who recorded His thoughts in the pages of the Old Testament.

Down through the ages, the prophecies of the coming Messiah became clearer, more detailed, more specific. The prophet Micah predicted His birth in the town of Bethlehem (Mic. 5:2). The prophet Isaiah foretold His virgin birth (Isa. 7:14), His anointing by the Holy Spirit (11:2), His message of good news (61:1), His miracles (35:5-6), and His rejection and death (53).

The prophet Zechariah predicted that He would enter Jerusalem as a king, riding on a donkey (Zech. 9:9), and that He would be "pierced" (as by a spear or by the nails of the cross; 12:10). The prophet Daniel predicted that He would be presented to Israel as king 173,880 days after the decree to rebuild the city of Jerusalem (Dan. 9:24-27).

The Psalms predicted His rejection (Ps. 118:22) and the piercing of His hands and feet along with other specific details of His crucifixion (22; 34:20; 69:21). The Psalms also predicted His resurrection (16:10) and His ascension into heaven (68:18; 110:1). And this list barely scratches the surface of the hundreds of Old

Testament prophecies which clearly identified Jesus of Nazareth as the promised Messiah and Deliverer.

Finally, the long-awaited, long-predicted moment arrived, and the baby Jesus was born to a virgin in the little Judean town of Bethlehem. The child grew to become a man. And that Man fulfilled all of the Old Testament prophecies—including the very first Old Testament prophecy, in which God told the serpent in the Garden of Eden, "And I will put enmity between you and the woman, and between your offspring and hers; he will crush your head, and you will strike his heel" (Gen. 3:15).

Jesus came and Satan struck His heel as He hung up on the cross at Calvary. But when He died and rose again, Jesus crushed the head of the serpent. He destroyed the curse of sin. He set humanity free from the fear of death. He opened the gates of heaven, so that all who believe in Him can enter in.

Spiritual "Gene Therapy"

In the Book of Romans, the apostle Paul reminds us that the genetic disorder of sin is always at work within our bodies. He wrote, "What a wretched man I am! Who will rescue me from this body of death?" (7:24).

We want to do good, yet the destructive effects of the sin disorder are constantly at work in our lives. Sin is not just something we *do*; it is a part of *who we are* as descendents of Adam and Eve. We are genetically predisposed to rebel against our Creator.

Our God is a righteous, holy, and just God, and we stand guilty before Him. The court of heaven declares that if we violate His laws (and we can't help but do so), then we will spend eternity separated from Him.

Many people find God's judgment difficult to accept. They refuse to acknowledge the awfulness of their own sin. "I'm a good person," they say. "Sure, I sin from time to time. But on the whole, I think my good deeds probably outweigh the bad. If I do enough good works, God will accept me."

But that is not how He sees it. His Word tells us that we can never do enough good works to counterbalance the weight of our sin. We can never hope to pay for our sins. We can never make ourselves acceptable to God by our own efforts. We can't earn His approval or work our way to heaven.

Remember, "good works" are the essence of every other religion on earth. All other religions involve striving to earn God's favor, striving to achieve moral perfection. We see this in the Jewish ceremonial law, the eightfold path of Buddhism, the Hindu doctrine of karma, and the Sharia law of Islam.

But the essence of Christianity is not human effort. Instead, it is God's grace. The concept of grace is unique to Christianity. It is not found in any other religious belief system. The doctrine of grace not only teaches that we don't *need* to earn our way to heaven; it teaches that it's *impossible* to earn our way to a heaven. The apostle Paul put it this way: "For it is by grace you have been saved, through faith—and this not from yourselves, it is the gift of God—not by works, so that no one can boast" (Eph. 2:8-9).

So it is a tragic and fatal error to believe, "I have lived a good life. I don't need to be saved." At the same time, it is also a tragic and fatal error to believe, "I have lived such a sinful life that I can *never* be saved."

People have said to me, "Michael, you have no idea how sinful I am. I have lived a wretched life. I'm a slave to sin. God cannot possibly forgive someone like me. I'm doomed to a life of guilt and shame—and I know that when I die, I'm destined for hell."

If that is how you feel, I want you to understand that God's grace is greater than any sin you have committed. Where did you get the idea that your ability to sin exceeds your heavenly Father's ability to forgive? Instead of focusing on yourself and your sin, focus on God and His love for you. Instead of focusing on your own past, focus on the bright and amazing future He wants to give you.

No one could ever earn his or her way to heaven. We are all under the curse of Adam's sin, and we are all unworthy of salvation. But no matter how far we have fallen into the depths of sin, we cannot fall beyond the reach of God's love and grace. He has forgiven, redeemed, and restored sinners of every kind—blasphemers, murderers, robbers, slave-traders, adulterers, and worse. Nothing you have done comes as a surprise to God. He is ready to receive you—yes, even you!

God has reached down to us. He has given us the gift of His Son, a gift of His extravagant grace. All He requires of us is that we accept that gift through faith.

ALL-ENCOMPASSING—AND TOTALLY FREE

We all were born with an eternal debt—a debt we can never repay through good works. In fact, the Bible tells us that the wages of sin is death (Rom. 6:23). But thank God, He has provided the way to repay our debt and save us from eternal death! In His love and grace to us, God sent His own Son Jesus to die on a Roman cross to rescue us from our sin. Jesus, God's sacrifice of Himself on our behalf, died voluntarily—His heart bursting with love and compassion for you and me.

As the Bible tells us, "For God so loved the world that he gave his one and only Son, that whoever believes in him shall not perish but have eternal life" (John 3:16). Think about it: the only One ever born without the debt of sin hanging around His neck was Jesus. Yet He is the only one qualified to take your place and mine—the only One who can pay our debt. Dying on the cross, He set us free from the power of sin. Once we accept the gift of the Father's grace, three amazing things take place:

1. *God delivers us from the defeat of the past.* As children of Adam, we are born dead—spiritually dead. All of our efforts to make ourselves acceptable to God

are doomed to defeat. But His grace erases the sins of the past, delivers us from death, and turns defeat into victory. His grace heals the "dis-grace" of our genetic sin disorder and makes us not just children of Adam, but God's adopted heirs.

2. *God gives us a victorious life in the present.* As Paul tells us, "But because of his great love for us, God, who is rich in mercy, made us alive with Christ even when we were dead in transgressions—it is by grace you have been saved" (Eph. 2:4-5). We were dead because of our genetic sin disorder, but God made us alive with Christ—truly a radical transformation! As a result of being alive with Him, the "sin genes" we inherited from Adam no longer control our daily lives.

Yes, we still are tempted—and yes, we still sin. But now our desire is to serve God. He makes His power available to us, day by day and hour by hour through His Holy Spirit. We can call upon His Spirit to set us free at every moment, whenever we are tempted. The apostle Paul reminds us, "And God raised us up with Christ and seated us with him in the heavenly realms in Christ Jesus" (Eph. 2:6). That is a present-moment promise, not a future promise. *At this very moment* we are connected to a heavenly source of power which enables us to live each day as God intended.

God's grace is a gift He gives us *now*. It is a gift He renews day by day and moment by moment. We don't have to work up more faith. Even our faith is a gift from God. All we have to do is accept this gift and exercise the faith He gives us. We can't take credit for God's grace. All we can do is give thanks for His gifts.

3. *God gives us a thrilling future.* In fact, He gives us *two* futures.

First, God gives us a bright future in this life. He makes our daily lives meaningful and purposeful. We no longer merely exist, but we truly *live* to serve Him. The good works we do in service to Him will never be lost or wasted. As Paul tells us, "For we are God's workmanship, created in Christ Jesus to do good works, which God prepared in advance for us to do" (Eph. 2:10).

Our good works do not save us, but they do give our lives a sense of purpose. As we serve Him, we have the thrill of knowing that we are ambassadors and servants of the King of all creation. The work we do for Him is infinitely and eternally important.

Second, God gives us a future in eternity with Him. Nothing we experience on earth can compare with the blessings God has planned for us in heaven with Him. It will be an unending future of adventure, joy, and pleasure in His presence. Our eternal future with Him is what we truly long for throughout our lives.

Think back to the most perfect day you've ever experienced: hiking through Yosemite Park or the Grand Canyon, watching the most beautiful sunset imaginable, the moments of your wedding, the birth of your first child. Whatever you remember as that most perfect and thrilling moment of your life, an infinitely greater *eternity* awaits you in heaven with the Lord. Every great joy of this passing life is just a preview of the endless joys that await you in the presence of almighty God.

Past, present, and future. This life and the life to come. The grace of God transforms everything! When we truly know Him in an intimate and personal way, everything is changed.

The grace of God is all-encompassing—and it is totally free.

"Free?" you may ask. "How is that possible?"
Turn the page and find out.

6

The Last Word

One of the most powerful and moving words in the English language is "home." When you are home, you are warm, secure, and protected. You belong. You are loved. You have food to eat, a bed to sleep in, and a roof to keep out the rain. Those who value home the most are those who are farthest from it: a soldier overseas, a prisoner in a cell, a patient in a hospital bed, a runaway child in a strange city.

One of the best-known, best-loved stories in the Bible is of a runaway who wandered far from home. It's a story told by Jesus—the parable of the prodigal son and the loving father. Many people have heard of this so-called Prodigal Son without truly understanding what the word "prodigal" means. It's not a word we hear very often. "Prodigal" means wasteful, excessive, and reckless about spending money.

The story of the prodigal son is recorded in Luke 15:11-32. There, Jesus speaks of a willful, selfish young man who goes to his father demanding his entire inheritance on the spot.

The son wants the property that will be passed on to him after his father dies. In effect, he says, "Dad, I can't wait for you to die. I want what's coming to me now. Whatever you're going to leave me in your will, give it to me right this minute!"

THE DEPTHS OF DEGRADATION

The son's words were shocking and scandalous to the people who first heard Jesus tell this story. It was as if this young man had gone to his father and said, "Drop dead!" The son *insulted* his father, revealing what an ungrateful, self-centered, and insensitive young man he was.

Yet the father loved his son so much that, instead of taking offense, he gave the young man what he demanded—a staggering sum of money. Cash in hand, the son turned his back on his father and walked away, intending never to return home again. In spite of the young man's disrespect and insults, the father's love was undiminished. He stood at the door and watched his son leave home. He waved, but the rebellious boy never looked back.

The young man wandered off into a distant land, far from home. He spent his money on good food, the best wine, and the company of prostitutes. He shared his money with other people, and in the process he made many so-called "friends." He gave no thought to the future, nor to what would happen when the money ran out.

When his pockets were empty, he could no longer buy food or drink or the company of prostitutes. All of his so-called "friends" abandoned him. Penniless and friendless, he realized he was completely alone in a strange land. He had no home to go to and had wasted his inheritance.

Finally, he was forced to take a job feeding hogs. There was no job more demeaning and humiliating for a Jewish person than feeding pigs—animals which were not only filthy and disgusting, but ritually unclean according to the Jewish faith. Moreover, the young man was so hungry he resorted to eating the vile food meant for the pigs. The Prodigal Son had sunk as low as he could go.

In the depths of his degradation and shame, the young man thought of home. He remembered his father. He had always sneered at his father's old-fashioned values, his outdated preaching about hard work and thrift. But now all of his father's "old-fashioned and outdated" ideas were beginning to make sense. The harsh reality of life in a hog pen had caused him to see his father from a different perspective.

The young man realized that if he had not been so self-centered, he could still be living in his father's house, sitting at his father's table, enjoying three square meals a day. If only he could go home—but what right did he have to expect anything from his father now? He had insulted him and squandered his inheritance.

But where else could he go? Perhaps he could return home and *beg* to be taken back—not as a son, but as a mere servant. If his father threw him out in the street, he'd be no worse off than in these hog pens.

So the young man decided to go home. He had a little speech all planned: "Father, I have sinned against heaven and against you. I am no longer worthy to be called your son; make me like one of your hired men."

Long before the young man reached the front door, his father spotted him out in the distance. This tells us that the father must have gone out every day, watching for his son, hoping to see him, hoping to welcome him home. Jesus tells us that the father was filled with compassion for his son and "he ran to his son, threw his arms around him, and kissed him." In the original language of the New Testament, Jesus actually says that the father kissed his son eagerly and repeatedly.

Do you see how much this father loved his son? Just think of all the hurt this young man had inflicted! Yet the father loved him with an overflowing love. In fact, he shouted to his servants, "Quick! Bring the best robe and put it on him. Put a ring on his finger and sandals on his feet. Bring the fattened calf and kill it. Let's have a feast and celebrate! For this son of mine was dead and is alive again; he was lost and is found!"

THE RADICAL CONCEPT CALLED "GRACE"

Most of us, as we listen to the story, can identify with the son. We all know what it means to want our own way, to be headstrong and self-willed. And we all have suffered the consequences of our own foolish actions. We are well-acquainted with the sting of regret. So it's easy to put ourselves in the sandals of the Prodigal Son.

Yet it's important to realize that this story is not about the son. It's primarily about the father. It's a story about God's free gift of grace—the gift of His totally undeserved goodness in our lives.

As we have already seen, the concept of grace, which is at the heart of the Christian faith, cuts across the grain of every other religion on earth. The people who first heard Jesus tell this story were steeped in Jewish ceremonial law, which they thought was about people trying to earn God's favor through observing rituals and rites. They failed to understand that Abraham was saved through faith.

When Jesus told this story, he presented the father as a man of "amazing grace"—a man who freely forgave his wayward son. Notice that the father never demanded an apology or an explanation. He never ordered the young man to make restitution or work off the debt. He never said, "I told you so," or "I hope this has taught you a lesson." No. The father received the son, kissed him repeatedly, and celebrated his return.

That is how our Father in heaven receives every returning, repenting child.

This story unveiled the radical nature of God's grace. No one in Jesus' audience had ever heard such a thing before. Their minds were steeped in religious ceremony and ritual. The idea that human beings could simply return home to God and be forgiven? Why, it was utterly unthinkable! Yet, when Jesus told the people about this loving and gracious father, a light broke through the clouds and illuminated their hearts.

Grace! This was new! This was a concept beyond human understanding! Only God in human flesh could introduce such a remarkable idea.

GRACE MAKES NO SENSE

The concept of grace made no sense in first-century Israel. In fact, grace makes no sense in our twenty-first-century culture today. Just ask yourself, *Why would the father receive the son back with open arms?* The young man deserved nothing but scolding and rejection. This unloving, ungrateful son had walked away from home, spurning his father's love, never looking back. He deserved no mercy, no welcome, no consideration whatsoever.

Why did the young man return? Because he had experienced a change of heart? No. He had come crawling back because he had nowhere else to go. He had run out of money. He had squandered everything his father had given him. He was hungry and destitute.

How did the father know his son had truly repented? How did he know the young man would not steal from him and then run off again? For all the father knew, his son had come back only to take advantage of him.

Logically, it was the height of foolishness to show grace and forgiveness to this young man. Grace made no sense to the first-century Jews who first heard the story of the prodigal son. And the story makes no more sense today.

A suburban father in North America would have no more reason to take back a rebellious and morally corrupt son today than a first-century father in the Middle East. In fact, in many homes across America and Europe, rebellious children are disowned and tossed out of the house by their parents for less serious offenses than this young man committed.

Grace makes no sense—yet grace is the heart of the Christian gospel.

Why would God offer forgiveness as a gift to people who willfully reject Him, rebel against Him, and wander away from Him? Why does God watch for us and pursue us and draw us to Himself?

The nature of grace is rooted in the nature of God. We can only understand grace when we understand who God is.

GRACE—NOT LENIENCY

There are two types of grace described in the Bible.

Theologians refer to the first form as "common grace." I prefer to call it "mercy." Common grace or mercy is the undeserved goodness that God freely gives to all human beings. Jesus spoke of this kind of grace when He said that "your Father in heaven . . . causes his sun to rise on the evil and the good, and sends rain on the righteous and the unrighteous" (Matt. 5:45). Everyone is permitted to enjoy the goodness of God's creation, whether they love Him or not.

The second form of grace is called "special grace." This is a grace that God gives to all who accept the gift of salvation through Jesus. This is the kind of grace the loving father gave to the Prodigal Son. It's the grace all of us are invited to receive from our heavenly Father—the inexhaustible riches of God's goodness that He showers upon us in spite of our wretchedness and sin.

When you receive Jesus as your only Savior and Lord, and God receives you in His open, loving arms, you will experience "special grace" from God. It's the grace that calms our fears, erases our guilt, and gives meaning to our lives.

Many people mistake God's grace for leniency or permissiveness. They seem to think the Lord looks upon our sin with a kind of easy-going tolerance, saying, "Oh well, they sinned again, but it's not really such a bad sin. I'll just look the other way and pretend not to notice." Or "He/She is a good person at heart."

But that's not how His grace works. God does not wink at sin. If you think He simply lets our sins slide unnoticed, you are making the same mistake Adam and Eve made in the Garden of Eden and the same mistake Cain made when he killed his brother in the field. Each of them thought they could sin and God wouldn't notice. They were wrong.

Nothing escapes His sight. God does not wink at sin. When we fall short of His glory, there is a price to pay. Grace is neither lenient nor permissive. Grace is not free, nor is it cheap. Grace is the costliest, most precious commodity in the universe. It cost God the infinitely precious lifeblood of His only Son.

There is only one basis on which any human being may receive God's grace: the death of Jesus Christ on the cross at Calvary. If Jesus had not obediently chosen to die upon the cross during that moment of decision in the Garden of Gethsemane, there would be no grace for anyone. We all would be dead in our sins.

The grace of God is His goodness toward us—goodness that is infinitely beyond what we truly deserve. That goodness and grace is made possible only through the death and resurrection of Jesus Christ.

God's grace is inexhaustible—but it is not infinite. In other words, there is no depth of sin which His grace cannot cover, but it will not go on forever. One day it will cease. When the grace of God comes to an end, judgment will take place.

Our God is an infinite and eternal God. He has no beginning and no end. But one day, there will be an end to His grace. So while His grace is still offered to us, freely and abundantly, let each of us accept it with gratitude. Let's revel in it, enjoy it, and thank God for it—but let us never take grace for granted or treat it as mere permissiveness or tolerance of sin.

The inexhaustible grace of God is the most exciting and exhilarating aspect of the Christian life. Receive it—and every facet of your life will be transformed.

The parable of the Prodigal Son and the loving father is filled with life-changing lessons. This story tells us that when we wander far away from our "home" with God, we bring suffering upon ourselves. When we live apart from Him, we waste our lives. All the things we think we want—money, excitement, sexual thrills, popularity, the freedom to do whatever we want—will eventually make us lonely and destitute. Our foolish choices will leave us in the "hog pen" of despair.

God, our loving Father in heaven, receives lost and undeserving sinners. He loves us even though we have insulted and mistreated Him. He loves us even though we have gone far away from Him and have wasted all of His blessings. God not only waits for us to return to Him, but He eagerly watches for us. He intensely desires that we come to Him and be saved.

Sin Produces Death

There are some important parallels between the parable of the Prodigal Son and the story of Adam and Eve. The Prodigal Son lived an ideal life while he was in his father's house. Everything the father owned was his to enjoy. Yet the son was not satisfied. He convinced himself that he needed to go far from home in order to live the kind of life that would make him happy and fulfilled.

In the same way, Adam and Eve lived an ideal life in the Garden of Eden. Everything God had created was theirs to enjoy. Yet they were not satisfied. Tempted by the serpent, they convinced themselves that they needed to taste the forbidden fruit in order to be happy and fulfilled.

Both the Prodigal Son and Adam and Eve sought their fulfillment in forbidden pleasures. Both spurned the blessings they already possessed. The son elevated his own wants and his own reason above his father's. Adam and Eve elevated their own wants and their own human reason above the will of their Creator. Just as the son thought he knew better than his father, Adam and Eve thought they knew better than their heavenly Father.

God told Adam and Eve not to eat the fruit of that one tree—but Eve put the forbidden fruit to a test. Perhaps she wanted to know what its texture was like, or how it tasted, or what its nutritional value might be. Perhaps she thought, "I have experienced every fruit which grows in this garden except one. I must experience the flavor of this fruit, even if it is forbidden."

So she bit into the fruit. She tasted it. It must have seemed sweet at first, as so many forbidden experiences do. She decided the serpent was right. God was wrong. So she took the fruit to her husband and offered him a taste, and both bought into the greatest lie.

The Prodigal Son also put the "forbidden fruit" to the test. He wanted to know what it was like to party all the time, to live his life as an endless riot of wine, women, and song. He wanted to experience every sensual pleasure, even if it was "forbidden fruit." So he took a big bite out of life and tasted it. It seemed sweet at first—but it ultimately left him impoverished, lonely, destitute, and eating food that reeked of the pig sty just to stay alive. He too bought into the greatest lie.

Many people feel as if they haven't lived until they have tasted all the forbidden experiences life has to offer. They think, *If God were really good, He wouldn't deny me the things I want. If I obey His commandments, I'm going to miss out on something good. My life won't be fulfilled. Since God's Word prohibits so many of my desires, God's Word must be wrong. There must be many ways to be accepted by Him. One of them is my way, not His.*

And that's why so many people end up enslaved by addictions and sinful habits they are powerless to break. They lose their reputations, their families, their careers, and their self-respect. In the end, they may even lose their lives and their immortal souls. Truly, the wages of sin is death (Rom. 6:23).

The moment Adam and Eve ate the fruit, they died—just as God had warned them. You might say, "No, they ate the fruit—and nothing happened!" But something *did* happen. After they ate, they hid themselves from God. They separated themselves from the intimate fellowship and friendship they once enjoyed with their Creator.

Why did they hide from God? Because they were spiritually dead!

Physical death would follow, but spiritual death came instantly. Their friendship with God was replaced by fear—fear of punishment, fear of God's disapproval. These are the signs of spiritual death.

Why didn't Adam and Eve experience physical death as well as spiritual death at the moment they ate the forbidden fruit? Answer: God's grace. Their Creator allowed them to continue living, even after their spiritual death, so they would have an opportunity to repent and return to Him.

In His grace, God also promised them a Savior who would come into the world, crush the serpent's head, and save Adam's race from sin and death. At the time, Adam and Eve couldn't understand all that God was telling them. The promise of the coming Messiah was shrouded in mystery.

But at least they understood that God was not going to leave them dead in their sins. Centuries would pass before the angel Gabriel would appear to Joseph and Mary, announcing that a child would be born to them—a child conceived by the Holy Spirit. The angel told Joseph and Mary to name their child

Jesus (*Yehoshua* in Hebrew, meaning "God delivers"), because He would save His people from their sins (Luke 1:26-31; Matt. 1:20-21).

Centuries before the child was born to Joseph and Mary, another couple, Adam and Eve, watched as God slaughtered an innocent animal in front of them and made garments to cover their shame. In this way, Adam and Eve were made to understand that innocent blood had to be shed so their sins could be forgiven. Through that animal sacrifice, God taught Adam and Eve that an innocent must die for the sins of the guilty.

Though Adam and Eve did not fully understand that lesson, they caught a glimpse of the amazing truth that the sinless Son of God would one day die in their place. That glimpse was enough. From that day forward, Adam and Eve placed their faith in the One who would come and save His people from their sins.

Now you are beginning to understand that Jesus did not just appear. He had been waiting ever since our first parents.

WHY DID JESUS HAVE TO DIE?

Why did it have to be that way? Why did Jesus have to suffer and die on that cross? Why didn't God simply shout from heaven, "All is forgiven—I'll wipe away your sins and pretend they never happened!"?

The reason we ask such questions is that we do not comprehend the awfulness of sin. We think, *I'm not a bad person. I didn't kill anybody. I didn't steal anything. I'm not an adulterer. I didn't commit any of the big sins. I know I'm not perfect—but who is? I haven't done anything that deserves death!*

If those are your thoughts, consider these facts: Adam didn't kill anybody. He didn't steal anything. (Who was there to steal from?) He didn't commit adultery. (His wife was the only woman on the planet.) He didn't commit any of the so-called "*big* sins." What was the sin that caused God to send the first man and his wife out of the Garden of Eden? Simply this: Adam chose his own way instead of God's. He wanted to be accepted by the Creator his way, not by God's *only* way.

That was all Adam did—and it was enough for God to exile him from paradise. And remember, Adam did exactly what people still do today. They choose their way instead of God's. Jesus said I am the only way, but many choose to believe the greatest lie and insist there are many ways to God.

Many people think the belief that "all paths lead to God" is a new and enlightened concept, but it's actually the oldest and greatest lie in the world. It's the Big Lie that was first told in the Garden of Eden and continues to be retold in books, magazines, and TV shows every day. It's the desire to please God *your* way, to be accepted by God *your* way, to think you can make it to heaven *your* way.

But there is only *one* way to God the Father. He opened that path to us through His Son Jesus. "I am the way and the truth and the life. No one comes to the Father except through me" (John 14:6).

That is God's last word on the subject of our salvation. We come to God the Father through Jesus alone. There is no other way.

So, are you ready to respond to God's love and grace in your life? Like the father who stood at the door—waiting and watching for his wayward son to come home—God waits for you. His arms are wide open. When you come to Him, He won't condemn you, no matter what you have done or how far you have strayed from home. He wants to receive you and welcome you home.

Are you ready to take that step? Then turn the page with me.

7

The Only Response

In his book *Love, Acceptance and Forgiveness*, Jerry Cook tells the story of a young drug dealer who was using illegal drugs with his girlfriend one day. He turned to her and said he would give anything to be rid of his addiction.

"I know how you can do that," she replied.

"How?"

"If you trusted in Jesus as your Savior, He would deliver you."

The young man was intrigued. Questioning her further, he learned that she had been raised in a Christian home and had learned the Bible throughout her childhood. But she always had been rebellious and resisted committing her life to Jesus Christ. The young man asked her what it meant to trust in Jesus as his Savior.

"I'm not going to tell you," she replied.

"Why not?"

"Because then you'll take off and be a Christian," she said. "And I won't see you anymore."

But the young man was sick and tired of his meaningless life. So he pushed and prodded, insisting that she tell him.

"All right," she said at last. "I'll tell you." So, even though this young woman was not a Christian and wanted nothing to do with Jesus, she explained God's plan of salvation to her drug-dealer boyfriend. She quoted the words of Jesus in John 3:16, "For God so loved the world that he gave his one and only Son, that whoever believes in him shall not perish but have eternal life." Then she explained that he should pray, admit that he was a sinner, and ask Jesus to take control of his life.

So the young man got up, went into another room, and talked to God. He asked Jesus to come into him and take over his life. Then he got up, said goodbye to his girlfriend, and walked out of that apartment. He never came back, and he never used drugs again.

And what happened to his girlfriend? As far as Jerry Cook knows, she never gave her life to Christ. Though she acknowledged that Jesus alone had the power to save a person from sin, she wanted nothing to do with Him.[1]

Even a rebellious and unwilling person can intellectually tell of the power of Jesus Christ, and how He alone can change hearts and lives. Jesus truly is the way, the truth, and the life. No one comes to the Father except through Him. When you hear that invitation, there is only one response you can make which leads to eternal life. Any other response will take you to a deadly future.

TOMORROW MAY BE TOO LATE

After Adam and Eve sinned, God promised to send a Deliverer—a Savior who would save people from their sins. Some 2,000 years ago, at God's appointed time, He fulfilled all of the prophecies through His Son Jesus Christ. Our Lord and Savior paid the price and endured the punishment for our sins—for the sins of everyone who comes to Him and receives Him. That is God's plan of salvation for you and me.

The day is coming when Jesus Christ will sit on His seat of judgment (2 Cor. 5:10). The entire human race will come before Him to be judged. There will be those who accepted God's gracious gift and those who chose their own way. Jesus will send away those who tried to twist and distort, water down, or rewrite His plan according to their own selfish desires.

Some people will say it's narrow-minded to believe that there is only one path to God. Yet Jesus Himself said, "Enter through the narrow gate. For wide is the gate and broad is the road that leads to destruction, and many enter through it. But small is the gate and narrow the road that leads to life, and only a few find it" (Matt. 7:13-14).

If you want to go to the Super Bowl™ or Disneyland™ or board an airplane, you have to pass through a narrow gate. You can't climb over a wall or slip through a back door or come up through a trap door. You can only enter through the narrow gate.

The road to God may be narrow, but it is clearly marked. Our heavenly Father has told you what you must do to be saved. His requirements are not burdensome. You do not have to crawl for ten miles on your knees through broken glass. You do not have to memorize any secret passwords. You do not have to flog yourself with a whip or cover yourself with sackcloth and ashes.

But you have to give up your mistaken notion that there are many ways to God.

Through the pages of this book, you have learned that your loving Father in heaven invites you to have fellowship with Him. So how will you respond? You must choose one of the only two possible responses to His invitation: accept it or reject it. Believe in Jesus and follow the narrow path, or turn your back on Him and go your own way.

You can say to God, "No, thanks. I prefer to go my own way. I like the broad path. I like to think there are many ways to heaven. I don't like Your path. I don't like the narrow way. Like Adam and Eve, like the Prodigal Son, I'm choosing to go my own way."

God has told you clearly what lies at the end of such a decision: destruction. Adam and Eve made that same decision and were exiled from the garden. The Prodigal Son made that same decision and ended up alone and destitute in a far-off country.

You may say, "I can reject God now and come back to Him later. I can go my own way for while. I can party and enjoy a sinful life now, and come back to Him later, just as the Prodigal Son returned home to his father."

Perhaps. But you are taking a terrible chance with your eternal destiny. You never know how much time you have on earth. Today could be the last day of your life. You may never get another opportunity to make this decision. Right now, if God is speaking to you and urging you to turn to Him and accept the gift He offers you, this may be the closest you'll ever come to making that decision. Tomorrow may be too late.

So I urge you to make the correct choice before another moment slips by: eternal life in heaven in the presence of almighty God. I don't make the rules. You don't make the rules. God makes the rules. He says there is only one way, and it's a narrow way. The name of that way is Jesus.

What will your choice be?

Be forewarned, there are many so-called pastors and preachers who now deny the fact that Jesus is the only way. They are not telling you the truth. Jesus is the Truth. Listen to Him.

INVITED INTO A RELATIONSHIP

It's important to take time out from the pressures of this life and think seriously about the meaning of life, the end of life, and the life *beyond* this one. From time to time, we need to ask ourselves, *What am I living for? What place does God have in my life? What will happen to me when I die?*

Most of us avoid those kinds of questions throughout our lives. We think there's plenty of time to think about such things. We think our lives will go on and on forever, and we'll never have to deal with questions of life and death.

"I'm just not a religious person," you might say. "I've been in churches before, and they're full of hypocrites. I want nothing to do with religion." Others say they are "spiritual." By that they mean their spirits are in tune with nature. But they too are misguided because they're looking for salvation away from God's only way.

The Lord Jesus would be the first to agree that there are hypocrites in the religious world. When He preached in ancient Palestine, He was repeatedly attacked by arrogant, self-important religious leaders—Jesus called them hypocrites to their faces. These same people later arranged to have him falsely accused and crucified.

But please understand this: God is not recruiting you to a *religion*. He is inviting you into a personal *relationship* with Him.

When Adam and Eve were created, they didn't have a religion. They didn't need a religion. They had a *relationship* with God. They were on intimate terms with Him, and He was their friend. And that's exactly the relationship God wants to have with you.

Does that mean you'll never be tempted again? No. Only Jesus was without sin. You will experience temptation—but you won't face it alone. God will send His Holy Spirit to live within you, to comfort you, and to shield you. Your life will demonstrate increasing evidence of the qualities the Bible calls "the fruit of the Spirit"—love, joy, peace, patience, kindness, goodness, faithfulness, gentleness, and self-control (Gal. 5:22-23).

God sends His Holy Spirit to every genuine believer. The Spirit will empower you to live for Him and seal you permanently as a child of God. As the Spirit gains more and more control of your life, He will reshape and redirect your life. You'll discover your true identity as a child of the living God.

When your earthly life is over, you'll have the indescribable experience of going home to be with your Father in heaven. There, you will experience life as it was meant to be lived when God placed Adam and Eve in the Garden of Eden. There will be no crime, no corruption there. You'll experience no suffering, no sickness, no sorrow. Death and pain will be no more—so of course, there will be no more tears.

Heaven will be a realm of adventure. God will have work for us to do there—exciting, meaningful service. Just as God gave Adam and Eve enjoyable work to do in the Garden of Eden, He will give us responsibilities to carry out in eternity. The book of Revelation tells us that God's people will serve Him in heaven throughout eternity (22:3). Believe me, there will not be one millisecond of boredom in heaven!

Yes, we will rest from our spiritual struggles. We will be free from guilt and regret. But we will be very busy serving Jesus as we reign forever with Him.

This world is impermanent and destined for destruction. But if we have placed our trust in Him, our citizenship is in the world to come—a permanent place called heaven.

No Finer Way to Live—and Die

The imperishable reality of heaven is what every human heart desperately longs for. We all want a home where we can live forever, experience endless joy in the Creator's presence, and be reunited with those we love. God Himself placed those desires within us, so that we would never be satisfied with anything less than eternity with Him. He wants to draw us into a relationship with Him, because only by joining our lives to His can we experience the eternal life He intended for us at creation.

God made us in His image so that we would be reflections of His intellect and spirit. He created you, me, and everyone else to experience friendship with Him. We are physical beings—but we are not *merely* physical. We are part of the spiritual realm, and we were created for heaven. We are restless and dissatisfied with life until we find our true destiny in Him. Only when our searching and wandering leads us home to the Father can we find the peace and belonging we seek.

As the Bible tells us, God has "set eternity in the hearts of men" (Eccles. 3:11). You and I were made for heaven. In his book *Heaven*, Randy Alcorn writes, "We are homesick for Eden. We are nostalgic for what is implanted in our hearts. It's built into us, perhaps even at a genetic level. We long for what the first man and woman once enjoyed—a perfect and beautiful Earth with free and untainted relationships with God, each other, animals, and our environment. Every attempt at human progress has been an attempt to overcome what was lost in the Fall."[2]

Down through history, God has sometimes allowed His followers to see a glimpse of heaven while they were still alive on earth. In the New Testament, we read the story of Stephen, who was stoned to death as the first Christian martyr. The account tells us that, as the enraged mob picked up stones and closed in around him, "Stephen, full of the Holy Spirit, looked up to heaven and saw the glory of God, and Jesus standing at the right hand of God. 'Look,' he said, 'I see heaven open and the Son of Man standing at the right hand of

God'" (Acts 7:55-56). As Stephen said this, the people rushed at him and stoned him to death.

Another follower of Christ who was granted a glimpse of heaven before he died was the popular and well-known preacher Dwight L. Moody (1837-1899). On November 16, 1899, Moody preached a sermon at a church in Kansas City, Kansas. Afterwards, he collapsed. Though doctors didn't know what caused the illness, Moody suffered from congestive heart failure. Sensing death approaching, Moody confided to his closest friends, "Soon you will read in the newspaper that I am dead. Don't believe it for a moment. I will be more alive than ever before."

Three days before Christmas, Moody lay on his deathbed. His family and friends gathered around him to say goodbye. Though he struggled to breathe, Moody had no fear of death. His eyes were alight with joy. Those who were with him said that he seemed to see things no one else could see. His last words were, "Earth recedes . . . heaven opens before me!"

Then he passed into the presence of our Lord.

There is no finer way to live—and no better way to die—than to live and die belonging to God's only way. It's an incredible blessing to know that your sins are forgiven, and that He has welcomed you with open arms—just as the loving father welcomed home the Prodigal Son.

So it's time to make a decision. Will you accept Him now? Your loving Father in heaven is ready and eager to accept you. All you need to do is say this simple prayer of decision and commitment:

> My Lord, my heavenly Father, thank You for Your love to me, a sinner. I know that I have violated Your moral law many times throughout my life. I mistakenly thought I could come to You my way. I am sorry and want to turn away from my sin and live for You. I invite Jesus to come into my life as Lord and Savior—to take control of my life from this day forward. Father, forgive my sin and receive me as Your child.

> Thank You for hearing my prayer and receiving me. Please seal this decision I've made and help me live the rest of my life for You. Live Your life through me. Guide me as I read Your Word. Thank You in Jesus' name. Amen.

If you prayed those words honestly and sincerely, then you have begun a new life of living for Jesus Christ. You are a child of the King, a member of His royal family.

Take note of this date. In the days, months, and years to come, the decision you just made will become more and more meaningful. Pray daily. Read God's Word. As you do so, you will grow stronger and deeper in your faith. Your friendship and fellowship with God will become more and more real to you.

As you grow in your Christian life, you'll discover an ever-deepening love for God and a growing desire to spend time with Him in prayer (Luke 18:1; Eph. 6:18). You'll discover the joy of getting to know other Christians and praying with them (Acts 2:42; 1 John 4:7-8). And you'll grow in your obedience to the Lord (John 14:15; 15:10).

Thank God every day for this gift of salvation He has given you. And don't keep it to yourself—tell other people around you what God has done for you. Be strengthened in your faith through daily prayer and Bible reading. And please, write to me and tell me about your decision to follow Jesus Christ. God bless you as you live for Him!

Dr. Michael Youssef
Leading The Way
P.O. Box 20100
Atlanta, Georgia, USA 30325

For more information about Leading The Way and its mission to passionately proclaim uncompromising Truth around the world, visit www.leadingtheway.org.

Notes

Introduction: Decide for Yourself

1. Richard Abanes, *Religions of the Stars: What Hollywood Believes and How It Affects You* (Bloomington, MN: Bethany House Publishers, 2009), p. 35.

2. The Big Lie

1. Deepak Chopra, *The Third Jesus: The Christ We Cannot Ignore* (New York: Random House, 2008), pp. 9-10.

4. The Indisputable Truth

1. Frederick A. Larson, "The Starry Dance," BethlehemStar.net, retrieved at http://bethlehemstar.net/dance/dance.htm.

2. Quoted by Emil Schürer (ed. by Géza Vermès, Fergus Millar, and Matthew Black), *The History*

of the Jewish People in the Age of Jesus Christ (Volume I) (Edinburgh: T & T Clark, Ltd., 1973), p. 441, Note 32.

3. Quoted by Gary R. Habermas, *The Historical Jesus: Ancient Evidence for the Life of Christ* (Joplin, MO: College Press, 1996), p. 188.

7. The Only Response

1. Jerry Cook with Stanley C. Baldwin, *Love, Acceptance and Forgiveness: Equipping the Church to Be Truly Christian in a Non-Christian World* (Ventura, CA: Regal Books, 1979), pp. 69-70.

2. Randy Alcorn, *Heaven* (Wheaton, Illinois: Tyndale, 2004), p. 77.